THE MARVEL OF
MOMS

THE MARVEL OF
MOMS

When Words Are Not Enough

Bonnie Louise Kuchler

WILLOW CREEK PRESS

Published by Willow Creek Press, Inc.
P.O. Box 147, Minocqua, Wisconsin 54548

Photo Credits:

p2 © Lisa & Mike Husar/TeamHusar.com; p5 © David & Micha Sheldon/age fotostock; p6 © Andrew Parkinson/age fotostock; p9 © ZSSD/Minden Pictures; p10 © Suzi Eszterhas/Minden Pictures; p13 © Solvin Zankl/NPL/Minden Pictures; p14 © Robert Harding Images/Masterfile; p17 © Thomas Dressler/age fotostock; p18 © Lisa & Mike Husar/TeamHusar.com; p21 © ARCOR Siegel/age fotostock; p22 © George Sanker; p25 © Jane Burton/NPL/Minden Pictures; p26 © Suzi Eszterhas/Minden Pictures; p29 © ZSSD/Minden Pictures; p30 © J & C Sohns/age fotostock; p33 © M. Woike/age fotostock; p34 © Charlie Summers/NPL/Minden Pictures; p37 © Thomas Dressler/age fotostock; p38 © George Sanker; p41 © Duncan Usher/Foto Natura/Minden Pictures; p42 © Richard Du Toit/Minden Pictures; p45 © FLPA/Elliott Neep; p46 © Jean-Paul Ferrero/Auscape/Minden Pictures; p49 © Beate Konstantinou/age fotostock; p50 © Matthias Breiter/Minden Pictures; p53 © Lisa & Mike Husar/TeamHusar.com; p54 © S. Sailer/A. Sailer/age fotostock; p57 © George Sanker; p58 © Yva Momatiuk & John Eastcott/Minden Pictures; p61 © Carol Walker/NPL/Minden Pictures; p62 © Jerome Gorin/age fotostock; p65 © Photoshot/age fotostock; © p66 FLPA/Malcolm Schuyl/Minden Pictures; p69 © Michael & Patricia Fogden/Minden Pictures; p70 © M. Delpho/age fotostock; p73 © Mitsuaki Iwago/Minden Pictures; p74 © Laurie Campbell/NPL/Minden Pictures; p77 © Suzi Eszterhas/Minden Pictures; p78 © Gerry Ellis/Minden Pictures; p81 © Michael Breuer/age fotostock; p82 © Adriano Bacchella/NPL/Minden Pictures; p86 © Cyril Ruoso/JH Editorial/Minden Pictures; p89 © Juniors Bildarchiv/age fotostock; p90 © Juniors Bildarchiv/age fotostock; p93 © T.J. RICH/NPL/Minden Pictures; p94 © Duncan Usher/ Foto Natura/Minden Pictures; p96 © Winfried Wisniewski/age fotostock

Design: Donnie Rubo
Printed in China

For my mom.
After 90 years of life, her strength
is waning and her memory is fading,
but there is absolutely nothing
feeble about her love for her kids.

Mom, my first home was
tucked beneath your heart,
and things haven't changed
all that much. Wherever your heart is,
will always feel like home to me.
—Bonnie

A mom has senses worthy of a superhero.
She sees what's happening behind her,
hears what isn't said,
feels what her children feel,
and smells anything that can multiply on its own.
With this super-sensitivity, a mom
could easily blow a gasket.
Unless, of course, she taps into another super sense...
her sense of humor.

*Life began with waking up
and loving my mother's face.*

—GEORGE ELIOT (1819-1880), ENGLISH NOVELIST

Becoming a mother is a cosmic event.
The center of the universe shifts,
and all life revolves around a
tiny, new heavenly body.

—BONNIE LOUISE KUCHLER

*The greatest forces in the world
are not the earthquakes and the
thunderbolts. The greatest forces
in the world are babies.*

—DR. E. T. SULLIVAN

*I had crossed over to a strange new world,
a world where another person's life
literally depended on me...
and this sense of being in a strange
land was all the more jarring since,
of course, I hadn't left home.*

—ANDREA BUCHANAN, US AUTHOR

Who was this tiny trusting baby who alternately screamed until my nerves were raw and snuggled until my heart broke from joy.

—ELIZABETH SOUTTER SCHWARZER, US JOURNALIST AND COLLEGE INSTRUCTOR

*The first steps
of a new mother
are much like
those of a baby...
wobbly.*

—BONNIE LOUISE KUCHLER

When mom gets chilly,
everybody puts on a sweater,
and when mom gets tired,
everybody takes a nap...
When mom is on a diet,
everybody starves.

—TERESA BLOOMINGDALE, US AUTHOR AND HUMORIST

We have a knack for feeling guilty over almost anything related to motherhood.

—TRISHA ASHWORTH AND AMY NOBILE, US AUTHORS

Some mothers are kissing mothers
and some are scolding mothers,
but it is love just the same,
and most mothers kiss and scold together.

—PEARL S. BUCK (1892-1973), US AUTHOR

Our mothers
always remain the strangest,
craziest people we've ever met.

—MARGUERITE DURAS (1914-1996), FRENCH WRITER AND FILM DIRECTOR

The phrase "working mother" is redundant.

—JANE SELLMAN, US WRITER

Motherhood...
Never being number
one in your list of priorities
and not minding at all.

—JASMINE GUINNESS, IRISH MODEL AND FASHION DESIGNER

Even when her emotions pitch and roll,
even when her body feels like a slug,
even when her heart is
breaking, the love of a mother
is never exhausted.

—BONNIE LOUISE KUCHLER

*One of the perks
of motherhood is
how often you get
to see the sunrise.*

—BONNIE LOUISE KUCHLER

If evolution really works, how come mothers have only two hands?

—ED DUSSAULT, HUMORIST

Motherhood improves your listening skills.

—BONNIE LOUISE KUCHLER

When you are a mother,
you are never really
alone in your thoughts.

—SOPHIA LOREN (B. 1934), ITALIAN ACTRESS

*The bond between mother and child
is a mix of love, trust, and superglue.*

—BONNIE LOUISE KUCHLER

My mom is literally a part of me. You can't say that about many people, except relatives and organ donors.

—CARRIE LATET, WRITER AND POET

Moms need time out too.

—BONNIE LOUISE KUCHLER

She never quite leaves her children at home,
even when she doesn't take them along.

—MARGARET CULKIN BANNING (1891-1982), US AUTHOR

Tell a mother not to worry?
You might as well hush an earthquake.

—BONNIE LOUISE KUCHLER

*When your mother asks,
"Do you want a piece of advice?"
it is a mere formality. It doesn't
matter if you answer yes or no.
You're going to get it anyway.*

—ERMA BOMBECK (1927-1996), US WRITER AND HUMORIST

*It is quite surprising
how many children survive
in spite of their mothers.*

—NORMAN DOUGLAS, US AUTHOR

Nothing is quite as hard as helping a person develop his own individuality, especially while you struggle to keep your own.

—MARGUERITE KELLY AND ELIA PARSONS, US AUTHORS

Children are... people to be unfolded.

—JESS LAIR, PH.D. (1926-2000), US AUTHOR AND PROFESSOR

*Mama exhorted her children
at every opportunity to
"jump at de sun."
We might not land on the sun,
but at least we would get off the ground.*

—ZORA NEALE HURSTON (1891-1960), US AUTHOR AND ANTHROPOLOGIST

People always talked about a mother's uncanny ability to read her children, but that was nothing compared to how children could read their mothers.

—ANNE TYLER (B. 1941), US NOVELIST

Don't worry that children never listen to you; worry that they are always watching you.

—ROBERT FULGHUM (B. 1937), US AUTHOR

I learned your walk, talk, gestures and nurturing laughter. At that time, Mama, had you swung from bars, I would, to this day, be hopelessly, imitatively, hung up.

—DIANE BOGUS, PH.D., US POET

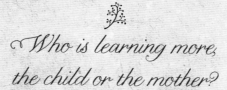

Who is learning more,
the child or the mother?

—BONNIE LOUISE KUCHLER

*The real menace in dealing
with a five-year-old is that
in no time at all you begin to
sound like a five-year-old.*

—JEAN KERR (B. 1923), US AUTHOR AND PLAYWRIGHT

Before kids, I actually held on to the illusion that there was some sense of order to this universe of ours.

—SUSAN LAPINSKI, US AUTHOR AND EDITOR

Never underestimate a child's ability to get into more trouble.

—UNKNOWN

Do not, on a rainy day, ask your child what he feels like doing, because I assure you that what he feels like doing, you won't feel like watching.

—FRAN LEBOWITZ (B. 1950), US AUTHOR

"There is no point at which you can say, "Well, I'm successful now. I might as well take a nap."

—CARRIE FISHER (B. 1956), US ACTRESS AND NOVELIST

A mother needs
fortitude
and courage
and tolerance
and flexibility
and patience
and firmness
and nearly every
other brave
aspect of the
human soul.

—PHYLLIS MCGINLEY (1905-1978) US WRITER AND POET

*Motherhood is something you
love every other minute of.*

—BONNIE LOUISE KUCHLER

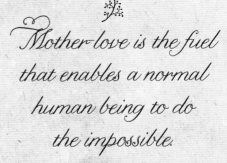

*Mother-love is the fuel
that enables a normal
human being to do
the impossible.*

—MARION C. GARRETTY (B. 1917), US WRITER

If love is a single flower,
then mother-love is a
meadow bursting
with blooms.

—BONNIE LOUISE KUCHLER

Mother-love is a beast burrowed deep in the heart, its fierce claws retracted within soft paws.

—BONNIE LOUISE KUCHLER

*It is a mother's caress that first
awakens a sense of security...
the first assurance that
there is love in the world.*

—DAVID O. MCKAY (1873-1970), PRESIDENT OF LDS CHURCH

*Mothers are the pivot
on which the family spins.
Mothers are the pivot
on which the world spins.*

- PAM BROWN, US WRITER